7912

The Evidence for the Resurrection of Jesus Christ

The Evidence for the Resurrection of Jesus Christ

Richard Riss

Legal, historical, and eyewitness evidence for the resurrection!

Bethany Fellowship INC.
MINNEAPOLIS, MINNESOTA 55438

*The Evidence for
the Resurrection of Jesus Christ*
by Richard Riss
Library of Congress Catalog Card Number 76-50978

ISBN 0-87123-134-4

DIMENSION BOOKS
Published by Bethany Fellowship, Inc.
6820 Auto Club Road
Minneapolis, Minnesota 55438

Printed in the United States of America

To Richard Taylor
Professor of Philosophy,
University of Rochester
and
to all people associated in any way with
the University of Rochester,
Rochester, N.Y.,
past, present and future

RICHARD RISS is presently a candidate for the Master of Christian Studies degree at Regent College, Vancouver, B.C., Canada. He did his undergraduate work at the University of Rochester, where he received his B.A. in Philosophy.

After his graduation from the university, he spent a year in Rochester as an associate staff member for Inter-Varsity Christian Fellowship at the University of Rochester.

This book was originally written as a paper for a course entitled, "Concepts of the Soul."

Contents

8

1

Introduction

According to Hebrew scriptures, there will be a bodily resurrection of the dead (Isa. 26:19). In the book of Daniel there is reference to an "awakening" of some to everlasting life and others to everlasting contempt (Dan. 12:2). According to the New Testament, also, there will be a bodily resurrection of the dead (Acts 26:8). John refers to a resurrection of life and a resurrection of judgment (John 5:28, 29). Acts mentions a resurrection of both the just and the unjust (Acts 24:15).

The Christians of the first century were convinced that Jesus of Nazareth had been resurrected from the dead (Acts 2:32). They considered Christ's resurrection to be an assurance that they, too, would be resurrected (1 Cor. 6:14). The resurrection of Christ also provided assurance that He would return to judge the world at the time of the resurrection (Acts 17:31), and that He was what He claimed to be (John 2:18-21).

The first-century Christians considered Jesus to be the "first fruits" of the resurrection (1 Cor. 15:20, 23). They expected that their resurrected bodies would be similar in appearance (and in their physical properties) to the resurrection body of Christ (Phil. 3:21).

The resurrection of Jesus was the primary epistemological basis for the validity of Christianity. Paul claimed that, "If Christ has not been raised, then our preaching is in vain and your faith is in vain. . . . If Christ has not been raised, your faith is futile" (1 Cor. 15:14, 17).

Therefore, the validity of biblical claims concerning resurrection is dependent upon the extent of the evidence for the historicity of the resurrection of Christ. It will be valuable, therefore, to examine the evidence.

Any thorough examination of the evidence for the historicity of the resurrection of Christ would take years of painstaking research. Since the information within this paper will only scratch the surface, it might be worthwhile to take note of what some prominent scholars have found who have taken the time to research the question thoroughly.

In the early eighteenth century, two individuals at Oxford University were determined to attack the very basis of Christianity. Lord George Lyttleton set out to prove that Saul of Tarsus had never been converted to Christianity; and Dr. Gilbert West, to demonstrate that Jesus had never risen from the dead. Later, when they met to discuss their findings, each found that the other had come independently to the conclusion opposite to that which he had set out to establish.[1] They collaborated in writing a book entitled *Observations on the History and Evidences of the Resurrection of Jesus Christ.*[2] On the flyleaf of the volume appeared the statement, "Blame not before thou hast examined the truth."

A prominent physician of the nineteenth century, David Nelson, was impressed with the levelheadedness of lawyers examining the evidence. He wrote:

> I do not know why it is so, but it is the result of eighteen years' experience, that lawyers, of all those with whom I have examined, exercise the clearest judgment, whilst investigating the evidences of Christianity. . . . I am unable to account

---

1. Michael Green, *Man Alive!* (Downers Grove, Ill.: Inter-Varsity Press, 1967), pp. 55-56.
2. Gilbert West and Lord George Lyttleton, *A Defence of the Christian Religion*, 1748.

for the fact, yet, so it is, that the man of law excels. He has, when examining the evidences of the Bible's inspiration, shown more *common sense* in weighing proof and appreciating argument, where argument really existed, than any other class of men I have ever observed. ... they look surprised for a moment when they are told they are *ignorant* of Bible literature; but when they do read thoroughly, and examine faithfully, they are better than ordinary judges of what is weakness, or what is force in reason.[3]

At the same time, Dr. Simon Greenleaf of Harvard Law School wrote his celebrated work, *A Treatise on The Law of Evidence* (1842), which is "still considered the greatest single authority on evidence in the entire literature of legal procedure." [4] Four years later, Greenleaf wrote a book examining the value of the testimony of the apostles to Christ's resurrection, the full title of which was *An Examination of the Testimony of the Four Evangelists by the Rules of Evidence Administered in the Courts of Justice*,[5] which soon became one of the

---

3. David Nelson, *The Cause and Cure of Infidelity* (New York: American Tract Society, 1841), p. 117.

4. Wilber M. Smith, *Therefore, Stand: Christian Apologetics* (W. A. Wilde Company, 1945), p. 423.

5. Simon Greenleaf, *The Testimony of the Evangelists* (A. Maxwell and Son, 1847).

most significant works of the nineteenth
century on the truthfulness of Christianity.

Concerning lawyers, Charles G. Finney
wrote:

> I have always been particularly interested
> in the salvation of lawyers, and all men
> of the legal profession. To that profession
> I was myself educated. I understood pretty
> well their habits of reading and thinking,
> and knew that they were more certainly
> controlled by argument, by evidence and
> by logical statements than any other class
> of men. I have always found, wherever I
> have labored, that when the Gospel was
> properly presented, they were the most
> accessible of men; and I believe it is true
> that, in proportion to their relative num-
> ber in any community, more have been
> converted than of any other class. I
> have been particularly struck by this, in
> the manner in which a clear presentation
> of the Law and the Gospel of God will
> carry the intelligence of judges, men who
> are in the habit of sitting and hearing tes-
> timony and weighing argument on both
> sides.[6]

Lord Caldecote, Lord Chief Justice of
England, has written:

> My faith began with and was founded on

6. Irwin H. Linton, *A Lawyer Examines the Bible*
(Grand Rapids, Mich.: Baker Book House, 1943), p.
14.

what I thought was revealed in the Bible. When, particularly, I came to the New Testament, the Gospels and other writings of the men who had been friends of Jesus Christ seemed to me to make an overwhelming case, merely as a matter of strict evidence, for the facts therein stated. ... The same approach to the cardinal test of the claims of Jesus Christ, namely, His resurrection has led me as often as I have tried to examine the evidence to believe it as a fact beyond dispute.[7]

Recently, Dr. Frank Morrison, a British Journalist and lawyer, undertook to write a book in order to refute the myth of the resurrection of Christ. He travelled to Palestine to do some of his research. While there, he was slowly convinced of the historicity of Christianity by the force of the evidence he encountered. The book that he has written concerning the evidence begins with a chapter which is significantly entitled, "The Book that Refused to be Written."[8]

A lawyer in Washington who is a member of the bar of the Supreme Court of the United States wrote a book in 1943 entitled,

---

7. *Ibid.*, p. 11.

8. Frank Morrison, *Who Moved the Stone?* (Downers Grove, Ill.: Inter-Varsity Press), p. 9.

A Lawyer Examines the Bible. In this semi-autobiographical book, he discusses many of his personal experiences with others in the law profession concerning the New Testament Evidences. He writes:

> I urge upon my fellow lawyers especially that they give themselves at least once before they die the benefit of their own skilled professional services in examining, by every acid test known to the law, the evidence and reasoning in support of the formally recorded opinions of many of the most famous members of our learned and skeptical profession that a thing proved beyond a reasonable doubt is the claim of the Christian religion and the Holy Bible to be in deed and in fact the one religion and book with the inspiration and sanction of the Almighty God behind them.[9]

Dr. J.N.D. Anderson, Professor of Oriental Law and Director of the Institute of Advanced Legal Studies at the University of London, wrote a book in 1969 entitled *Christianity: The Witness of History*, which is an examination of the evidence for the life, death and resurrection of Jesus Christ. In his book he writes:

> . . . it seems to me inescapable that any-

---

9. Irwin H. Linton, *op. cit.*, p. 13.

one who chanced to read the pages of the New Testament for the first time would come away with one overwhelming impression—that here is a faith firmly rooted in certain allegedly historical events, a faith which would be false and misleading if those events had not actually taken place, but which, if they did take place, is unique in its relevance and exclusive in its demands on our allegiance.[10]

At the conclusion of his book, J.N.D. Anderson writes:

We could never make ourselves one with a holy God, but God in Christ offers to come into our lives and our hearts, if we invite him in as Saviour and Lord, and to share with us his own divine life. Nor is this mere wishful thinking; it is sober fact, to which I and many others can testify in our experience.[11]

In a speech delivered at the University of Rochester in the spring of 1971 on the evidence for the historicity of the resurrection of Christ, Josh McDowell cited the example of Thomas Arnold, who was famous headmaster of Rugby for fourteen years, and who held the chair of Modern History at Oxford. Noted for his famous

10. J.N.D. Anderson, *Christianity: The Witness of History* (London: Tyndale Press, 1969), p. 13.

11. *Ibid.*, p. 108.

three-volume *History of Rome*, he made this extravagant claim:

> I know of no one fact in the history of mankind which is proved by better and fuller evidence of every sort, to the understanding of a fair inquirer, than the great sign which God has given us that Christ died and rose again from the dead.[12]

John Warwick Montgomery, when an undergraduate philosophy student at Cornell University, encountered what he calls the "crucial problem-area" of the historical evidence for the claims of Christianity, and became a Christian as a result.[13]

C. S. Lewis, Professor of Mediaeval and Renaissance literature at Cambridge University until his death in 1963, says, concerning his conversion to Christianity, that:

> The real clue had been put into my hand by that hard-boiled athiest when he said, "Rum thing, all that about the Dying God seems to have really happened once." [14]

12. Thomas Arnold, *Sermons on the Christian Life: Its Hopes, Its Fears, and Its Close*, 6th ed. (London, 1859), p. 324, as quoted by Wilber M. Smith, *Therefore Stand: Christian Apologetics* (W. A. Wilde Company, 1945), p. 426.

13. John Warwick Montgomery, *History and Christianity* (Downers Grove, Ill.: Inter-Varsity Press, 1964), p. 13.

14. C. S. Lewis, *Surprised by Joy* (New York: Harcourt, Brace and World, 1955), p. 235.

Elsewhere, C. S. Lewis has written that he was brought "kicking and struggling" into the kingdom of God by the historical evidence.[15]

In his book, *The Case for Biblical Christianity*, E. J. Carnell writes:

> It is extremely difficult to understand why it is necessary to antagonize faith's relation to rational evidences. Kierkegaard started off with a completely false prejudice in supposing that inwardness is jeopardized when the mind is satisfied with the consistency of objective evidences. ... In our daily living, we *proportion* our inward response to the certainty of the evidences. ... While faith may involve a cordial commitment of the whole man to Jesus Christ, it is a passion which is drawn out by objectively measurable evidences. Whenever spirit is satisfied that the evidences are sufficient, it rests in truth.[16]

---

15. C. S. Lewis, *Surprised by Joy* (London: Fontana Books, 1959), p. 183. See also John Warwick Montgomery, *History and Christianity* (Downers Grove, Ill.: Inter-Varsity Press, 1964), p. 13.

16. E. J. Carnell, *The Case for Biblical Christianity* (Grand Rapids, Mich.: Eerdmans, 1969), pp. 55-56. See also Cark H. Pinnock, *Set Forth Your Case: Studies in Christian Apologetics* (Chicago: Moody Press, 1971), pp. 92-94.

2

The Date and Manuscript Attestation of the Documents of the New Testament*

Most scholars date the New Testament documents as follows:

Matthew, A.D. 85[1]
Mark, A.D. 60-65[2]

---

*Although the research in chapters two and three is original, many of the references used are the same as those originally cited by F. F. Bruce in *The New Testament Documents: Are They Reliable?* (Downers Grove, Ill.: Inter-Varsity Press, 1943), chapters II and VII.

1. Burnett Hillman Streeter, *The Four Gospels, A Study of Origins* (New York: The Macmillan Co., 1925), p. 487, and Vincent Taylor, *The Gospels, A Short Introduction* (London: Epworth Press, 1930), p. 96.

2. Burnett Hillman Streeter, *op. cit.*, p. 487, and Vincent Taylor, *op. cit.*, p. 59.

Luke, A.D. 80-85[3]
John, A.D. 90-95[4]
Pauline Epistles, A.D. 48-64[5]

It should be emphasized concerning the four Gospels that these are the latest possible dates of authorship, and that there are excellent reasons for earlier dating. For example, C. E. Raven writes:

> That Acts was written before St. Paul's trial at Rome seems a strong probability, and the case for a subsequent incorporation of Mark is not strong. The general habit of placing the Synoptic Gospels in the period A.D. 70-100 is inexplicable; for the evidence is weaker than the objections. They reflect a time before the scattering of the Palestinian Church and the digression of the local and conservative community, a time utterly unlike the age of experiment and syncretism which followed Nero's persecution and the sack of Jerusalem.[6]

Most scholars consider Luke and Acts to be two parts of one document.[7] The book

---

3. Vincent Taylor, *op. cit.*, p. 86.

4. *Ibid.*, p. 99.

5. F. F. Bruce, *The New Testament Documents: Are They Reliable?* (Downers Grove, Ill.: Inter-Varsity Press, 1943), pp. 13, 14.

6. Charles E. Raven, *Jesus and the Gospel of Love* (New York: Henry Holt and Co., 1931), p. 128.

7. Sir William M. Ramsay, *Luke the Physician* (New York: A. C. Armstrong and Son, 1908), p. 6.

of Acts gives a detailed account of the later portion of the life of the Apostle Paul, but ends abruptly without mentioning that Paul was tried in Rome and martyred under Nero in A.D. 64.[8] Therefore, it would be reasonable to date the Gospel of Luke and the book of Acts prior to A.D. 64.

The temple at Jerusalem was destroyed at A.D. 70, and the city was overtaken at that time.[9] The Jews and the Palestinian church were scattered, causing conditions totally different from the conditions which one would expect should exist at the time of the writing of such documents as these.

William F. Albright, who died in 1971, has been considered one of the world's foremost biblical archaeologists. He distinguished himself enough to have an article devoted to him in the 1966 edition of the *Encyclopaedia Britannica,* which states that he "considerably influenced the development of biblical and related near eastern scholarship." [10] In an interview with *Christianity Today* magazine, William F. Albright stated:

. . . in my opinion, every book of the New

8. John Warwick Montgomery, *History and Christianity* (Downers Grove, Ill.: Inter-Varsity Press, 1964), p. 35.

9. *Encyclopaedia Britannica* (Chicago: William Benton, 1966), XII, 1008.

10. *Ibid.*, I, 531.

Testament was written by a baptized Jew between the forties and eighties of the first century A.D. (very probably sometime between about 50 and 75 A.D.) [11]

This is the opinion of one who has taken into account all the considerations involved in making such a judgment. Being better informed of these considerations than almost anyone else in the world, having first-hand knowledge of them, his statement carries tremendous weight.

In the middle of the nineteenth century it was confidently asserted by the very influential Tübingen school that the four Gospels and the book of Acts did not exist before the thirties of the second century A.D. Yet at this time there was sufficient evidence to demonstrate that this assertion was completely unfounded as was shown by Lightfoot, Tregelles and Tischendorf, as well as others. Since that time, the amount of evidence has increased to the degree that the Tübingen views are no longer held by scholars.

The evidence for the New Testament writings is considerably greater than the

---

11. *Christianity Today,* VII, 359, January 18, 1963, "Toward a More Conservative View," interview with William F. Albright.

evidence for most classical works. Historians have protested vigorously against the excessive skepticism of theologians in dealing with the historical writings of the New Testament. Examples include Edvard Meyer, A. T. Olmstead,[12] William M. Ramsay[13] and Henry J. Cadbury.[14]

There are in existence over 4,000 Greek manuscripts of the New Testament, as well as 8,000 manuscripts of the Latin Vulgate and 1,000 of other early versions.[15] Some of the best and most important of the Greek New Testament go back to about A.D. 350. Two important manuscripts are the Codex Vaticanus in the Vatican Library in Rome and the Codex Sinaiticus in the British Museum.[16] From the four hundreds A.D.,

---

12. Edvard Meyer, *Ursprung Und Ayfänge Des Christentums* (Stuttgart: J. G. Cottaishe, 1962) and A. T. Olmstead, *Jesus in the Light of History* (New York: Charles Scribner's Sons, 1942).

13. William Ramsay, *Luke the Physician* (New York: A. C. Armstrong and Son, 1908).

14. Henry J. Cadbury, *The Book of Acts in History* (New York: Harper and Brothers, 1955).

15. A. T. Robertson, *An Introduction to the Textual Criticism of the New Testament* (New York: George H. Doran Co., 1925), p. 70. At the present time, there are about 5,000 Greek manuscripts of the New Testament.

16. F. F. Bruce, *The New Testament Documents: Are They Reliable?* (Downers Grove, Ill.: Inter-Varsity Press, 1960), p. 16.

we have the Codex Alexandrinus in the British Museum, and from a hundred years later, the Codex Bezæ in the Cambridge University library, which contains the Gospels and Acts in both Greek and Latin.[17]

The textual advantage of the New Testament documents over all other ancient manuscripts is that, in no other case is the interval of time between date of authorship and date of earliest extant manuscripts so short.[18] Furthermore, the number of extant manuscripts is far greater for the New Testament than for any other classical work.[19] For other ancient works, manuscript attestation is poor in comparison. For example, we have, of the seven surviving plays of Sophocles, four manuscripts that are of any value, the earliest being written in the eleventh century, 1400 years after the poet's death.[20] For Plato, we have twelve manuscripts, the earliest being written about 1300 years after his death.[21] The *History* of Thucydides has eight manu-

17. *Ibid.*, p. 16.

18. Frederic G. Kenyon, *Handbook to the Textual Criticism of the New Testament* (London: Macmillan and Co., 1901), p. 4.

19. *Ibid.*, p. 4.

20. F. W. Hall, *A Companion to Classical Texts* (Oxford: Clarendon Press, 1913), pp. 268-269.

21. *Ibid.*, pp. 259-260.

scripts, the earliest being written in the tenth century, 1300 years after his death,[22] and Heroditus also has eight manuscripts, the earliest being from the tenth century, again 1300 years after his death.[23] Yet there is no classical scholar who will doubt the authenticity of these works, despite the paucity of extant manuscripts and despite the gap of over 1,000 years between the time of authorship and the time the earliest extant manuscript was written.

Yet, in addition to the examples of the Greek manuscripts of the New Testament documents that have been mentioned, we have the Chester Beatty Biblical Papyri, containing eleven papyrus codices, three of which contain most of the New Testament writings. The first contains the four Gospels and Acts and was copied between A.D. 200 and 250, the second contains the letters of Paul and Hebrews and was copied at about the same time, and the third, which includes the book of Revelation, was copied about 50 years later.[24]

Another discovery consists of some papyrus fragments dated not later than

22. *Ibid.*, pp. 279-280.
23. *Ibid.*, pp. 237-238.
24. F. F. Bruce, *op. cit.*, p. 17.

A.D. 150 by papyrological experts, which consists of fragments of an unknown gospel and other early Christian papyri.[25]

An earlier fragment, dated on paleographical grounds around A.D. 130, is a papyrus codex containing John 18:31-33, 37f., which was found in Egypt in 1917.[26]

The papyrus Bodmer II, written about A.D. 200, contains the first 14 chapters of John with the exception of 22 verses and portions of the last seven chapters.[27]

Frederic C. Kenyon, who was keeper of manuscripts in the British Museum, wrote:

> But besides confirming the . . . authenticity of the canonical books, the new evidence tends to confirm the general integrity of the text as it has come down to us. . . . The interval then between the dates of original composition and the earliest extant evidence becomes so small as to be in fact negligible, and the last foundation for any doubt that the Scriptures have come down to us substantially as they were written has now been removed. Both the *authenticity* and the

25. H. Idris Bell and T. C. Skeat, *Fragments of an Unknown Gospel and Other Early Christian Papyri* (London: Trustees of the British Museum, 1935).

26. C. H. Roberts, *An Unpublished Fragment of the Fourth Gospel* (Manchester: The Manchester University Press, 1935).

27. F. F. Bruce, *op. cit.*, p. 18.

general integrity of the books of the New Testament may be regarded as finally established.[28]

In the writings of the early church fathers, we find extensive quotes from the New Testament. The letter of Barnabas, it is now agreed, could not be any later than A.D. 150 and might be as early as A.D. 70.[29] This letter quotes from Romans, Ephesians, and Hebrews, and demonstrates a knowledge of eight other New Testament books.[30] Although the dating for the *Didache* is not firmly established, there is good reason to believe that it was in circulation prior to A.D. 70.[31] The *Didache* demonstrates a knowledge of Matthew, Luke, Acts, Romans, 1 Corinthians and 1 Peter, and possibly Hebrews and Jude.[32] The *Epistle to the Corinthians* of

28. Sir Frederic Kenyon, *The Bible and Archaeology* (New York: Harper and Brothers, 1940), pp. 288-289.

29. Francis Glimm, *The Apostolic Fathers* (Washington, D.C.: The Catholic University of America Press, 1962), p. 187.

30. Committee of the Oxford Historical Society of Historical Theology, *The New Testament in the Apostolic Fathers* (Oxford: Clarendon Press, 1905), pp. 1-23.

31. Jean-Paul Audet, *La Didachè Instructions Des Apôtres* (Paris: Libraire Lecoffre, 1958), pp. 187-210.

32. *The New Testament in the Apostolic Fathers*, *op. cit.*, pp. 24-36.

Clement of Rome also had early circulation and popularity in the first century.[33] This letter quotes from Romans, 1 Corinthians, Hebrews and possibly Acts. Extensive familiarity with nine other New Testament books is demonstrated.[34] The letters of Ignatius of Antioch, all written before his death in about A.D. 117,[35] refer to Matthew, John, Romans, Galatians, Ephesians, Philippians, 1 Timothy, 2 Timothy, Titus, and possibly eleven other New Testament books.[36] Polycarp's Letter to the Philippians, written in A.D. 135,[37] quotes John, Acts, Romans, 1 Corinthians, 2 Corinthians, Galatians, Ephesians, Philippians, Colossians (?), 2 Thessalonians, 1 Timothy, 2 Timothy, Hebrews, James and 1 John.[38] Other early Christian writings (such as *The Shepherd of Hermas* and *II Clement*) contain extensive

---

33. Francis Glimm, *op. cit.*, p. 4.

34. *The New Testament in the Apostolic Fathers*, *op. cit.*, pp. 37-62.

35. Edgar J. Goodspeed, *The Apostolic Fathers* (New York: Harper and Brothers, 1950), p. 204.

36. *The New Testament in the Apostolic Fathers*, *op. cit.*, pp. 63-83.

37. Francis Glimm, *op. cit.*, p. 132.

38. *The New Testament in the Apostolic Fathers*, *op. cit.*, pp. 84-104.

quotations of the New Testament documents.[39]

From the writings of the Gnostic school of Valentinus which were recently discovered, we know that before A.D. 150 most of the books of the New Testament were well known among the people of this sect.[40]

A great deal of external evidence exists for the authenticity of the New Testament documents. Papias, bishop of Hierapolis about A.D. 130, writes the following on the basis of information obtained from the "presbyter" John:

> This also the Presbyter used to say, "When Mark became Peter's interpreter, he wrote down accurately, although not in order, all that he remembered of what was said or done by the Lord. For he had not heard the Lord nor followed Him, but later, as I have said, he did Peter, who made his teaching fit his needs without, as it were, making any arrangement of the Lord's oracles, so that Mark made no mistakes in thus writing some things down as he [Peter] remembered them. For to one thing he gave careful attention, to omit nothing of what he heard and to falsify nothing in this."

39. *Ibid.*, pp. 105-136.
40. F. F. Bruce, *op. cit.*, p. 19.

Now Matthew collected the oracles in the
Hebrew language, and each one inter-
preted them as he was able.[41]

Irenaeus was a student of Polycarp,
bishop of Smyrna, martyred in A.D. 156
after being a Christian for 86 years. Polycarp had been a disciple of the Apostle
John himself. Irenaeus had often heard
from Polycarp the eyewitness accounts of
Jesus received from John and others who
knew Jesus.[42] In *Adversus haerese*, III.

---

41. This quotation from Papias is cited in Eusebius'
Historica ecclesiastica, III. 39., reprinted in Roy J.
Deferrari, *Eusebius Pamphili Ecclesiastical History*
(New York: Fathers of the Church, Inc., 1953), p.
329.

42. Eusebius, *Ecclesiastical History*, Book 5, Chapter 20, reprinted in Roy J. Deferrari, *Eusebius Pamphili, Ecclesiastical History* (New York: Fathers of
the Church, Inc., 1953), p. 329.

Eusebius writes as follows:

In the letter to Florinus which we have mentioned above, Irenaeus again speaks of his as-
sociation with Polycarp, saying: " . . . so that
I can tell even the place where the blessed Polycarp sat and talked, his goings and comings,
and manner of his life, and the appearance
of his body, and the discourses which he gave
to the multitude, and how he reported his living
with John and with the rest of the Apostles who
had seen the Lord, and how he remembered
their words, and what the things were which
he heard from them about the Lord, and about
His teaching."

I (ca. 180), Irenaeus writes:

> Now these, all and each of them alike
> having the Gospel of God,—Matthew for
> his part published also a written Gospel
> among the Hebrews in their own lan-
> guage, whilst Peter and Paul were at
> Rome, preaching, and laying the founda-
> tion of the Church. And after their de-
> parture, Mark, Peter's disciple and inter-
> preter, did himself also publish unto us
> in writing the things which were preached
> by Peter. And Luke too, the attendant of
> Paul, set down in a book the Gospel
> preached by him. Afterwards John the
> disciple of the Lord, who also leaned on
> His Breast,—he again put forth his Gos-
> pel, while he abode in Ephesus in Asia.[43]

The high importance of this testimony
of Irenaeus is demonstrated in an article,
"The Irenaeus Testimony to the Fourth
Gospel" by Frank Grant Lewis.[44]

---

43. Irenaeus, *Against Heresies,* Book 3, Chapter
1, reprinted in John Keble, *Five Books of S. Irenaeus
Against Heresies* (London: Rivingtons, 1877), p. 204.

44. Department of Biblical and Patristic Greek,
University of Chicago, *Historical and Linguistic
Studies in Literature Related to the New Testament*
(Chicago: University of Chicago Press, 1909), Vol. 1,
pp. 451-514.

3

The Accuracy of Luke as a Historian

Luke, the friend and companion of Paul, is the author of the third Gospel and the Acts of the Apostles, which are really two parts of one continuous historical work.[1] Luke mentions three emperors by name—Augustus (Luke 2:1), Tiberius (Luke 3:1), and Claudius (Acts 18:2 and Acts 11:28). The birth of Jesus is fixed in the reign of the Emperor Augustus, when Herod the Great was king of Judaea, and Quirinius governor of Syria (Luke 1:5, 2:1f.). Luke elaborately dates by a series of synchronisms in the Greek historical manner the beginning of John the Baptist's ministry (Luke 3:1f.), just as the Greek historian Thucydides dates the formal outbreak of the Peloponnesian War in his *History,* book

---

1. F.F. Bruce, *op. cit.*, p. 80.

II. Luke accurately names the Roman governors Quirinius, Pilate, Sergius, Paullus, Gallio, Felix, and Festus, Herod the Great and a few of his descendants, including Herod Antipas the tetrarch of Galilee, the vassal-kings Herod Agrippa I and II, Berenice and Drusilla, Jewish priests such as Annas, Caiaphas, and Ananias, and Gamaliel, the great Rabbi and Pharisaic leader. An author relating his story to the wider context of world history must be careful, because he affords the reader abundant opportunities to test the degree of his accuracy. Not only does Luke take this risk, but he stands the test admirably. F. F. Bruce writes:

> One of the most remarkable tokens of his accuracy is his sure familiarity with the proper titles of all the notable persons who are mentioned in his pages. This was by no means such an easy feat in his days as it is in ours, when it is so simple to consult convenient books of reference. The accuracy of Luke's use of the various titles in the Roman Empire has been compared to the easy and confident way in which an Oxford man in ordinary conversation will refer to the Heads of Oxford colleges by their proper titles—the *Provost* of Oriel, the *Master* of Balliol, the *Rector* of Exeter, the *President* of Magdalen, and so on. A non-Oxonian like the

34

present writer never feels quite at home
with the multiplicity of these Oxford titles.
But Luke had a further difficulty in that
the titles sometimes did not remain the
same for any great length of time; a
province might pass from senatorial government to administration by a direct
representative of the emperor, and would
then be governed no longer by a procon-
sul but by an imperial legate (*legatus
pro prœtore*).[2]

F. F. Bruce gives multitudes of specific
examples of the incredible accuracy of
Luke as a historian.[3]

Among the incredible number of supposed mistakes of Luke that have since
been vindicated was the mention in Luke
3:1 of Lysanias the tetrarch of Abilene in
the fifteenth year of Tiberius (A.D. 27-28).
The only Lysanias of Abilene otherwise
known from ancient history was a king who
was executed by the order of Mark Antony
in 34 B.C. We now have archaeological evidence of a later Lysanias who had the status
of tetrarch. An inscription recording the
dedication of a temple reads, "For the sal-
vation of the Lords Imperial and their whole
household, by Nymphæus, a freedman of

Lysanias the tetrarch." The reference to "Lords Imperial," which was a joint title given only to the Emperor Tiberius and his mother Livia, the widow of Augustus, establishes the date of the inscription to between A.D. 14 and 29, the years of Tiberius' accession and Livia's death, respectively.[4]

In the book of Acts, chapters 27 and 28, Luke records a sea voyage from Palestine on which he was shipwrecked en route to Italy with Paul and his companions. H. J. Holtzmann describes this as "one of the most instructive documents for the knowledge of ancient seamanship."[5] James Smith of Jordanhill, an experienced yachtsman who was quite familiar with the part of the Mediterranean Sea on which Paul sailed, bears witness to the remarkable accuracy of Luke's account of each part of the voyage. He writes:

> I do not even assume the authenticity of the narrative of the voyage and shipwreck contained in the Acts of the Apostles, but scrutinise St. Luke's account of the voyage precisely as I would those of Baffin or

4. Edvard Meyer, *Ursprung Und Anfänge Des Christentums* (Stuttgart: J. G. Cottaishe, 1962), pp. 46-49.

5. H. J. Holtzmann, *Hand-Commentar zum Neuen Testament* (Freiburg: Akademische Verlagsbuchhandlung Von J.C.B. Mohr, 1889) pp. 420-426.

36

Middleton, or of any antient (sic) voyage of doubtful authority, or involving points on which controversies have been raised. A searching companion of the narrative, with the localities where the events so circumstantially related are said to have taken place, with the aids which recent advances in our knowledge of the geography and the navigation of the eastern part of the Mediterranean supply, accounts for every transaction—clears up every difficulty—and exhibits an agreement so perfect in all its parts as to admit but of one explanation, namely, that it is a narrative of real events, written by one personality engaged in them, and that the tradition respecting the locality is true.[6]

Concerning the accuracy of Luke as a historian, F. F. Bruce writes:

Now, all these evidences of accuracy are not accidental. A man whose accuracy can be demonstrated in matters where we are able to test it is likely to be accurate even where the means for testing him are not available. Accuracy is a habit of mind, and we know from happy (or unhappy) experience that some people are habitually accurate just as others can be depend-

---

6. James Smith, *The Voyage and Shipwreck of St. Paul* (London: Longman, Brown, Green and Longmans, 1848), pp.v-vi.

ed upon to be inaccurate. Luke's record entitles him to be regarded as a writer of habitual accuracy.[7]

Sir William Ramsay writes:

The present writer takes the view that Luke's history is unsurpassed in respect of its trustworthiness. At this point we are describing what reasons and arguments changed the mind of one who began under the impression that the history was written long after the events and that it was untrustworthy as a whole.[8]

Concerning the accuracy of Luke as historian, Henry J. Cadbury, a professor from Harvard University, writes,

The historical worth of the Acts of the Apostles is not to be expressed merely in such negative terms. In itself it often carries its own evidences of accuracy, of intelligent grasp of its theme, of fullness of information. Its stories are not thin and colorless but packed with variety and substance. There is reason for the modern scholar to ponder them carefully, to ex-

7. F. F. Bruce, *op. cit.,* p. 90. See also Sir William M. Ramsay, *The Bearing of Recent Discovery on the Trustworthiness of the New Testament* (London: Hodder and Stoughton, 1915), p. 80.

8. Sir William Ramsay, *The Bearing of Recent Discovery on the Trustworthiness of the New Testament* (London: Hodder and Stoughton, 1915), p. 81.

amine them in detail and to compare them point for point throughout the volume. . . . The data which throw light on the history in Acts are also the data which confirm its place in history. But there is a difference in the approach. To a large extent the material with which I shall deal is capable of an apologetic use. It can be cited to show that the author of Acts is dealing with facts and reality.[9]

9. Henry J. Cadbury, *The Book of Acts in History* (New York: Harper and Brothers, 1955), pp. 3, 4.

4

The Use of Literary Criticism

Many critics of the authenticity of documents included within the Old and New Testaments base their contentions upon principles of literary criticism. The use of modern higher biblical criticism, employing the methods of literary criticism in establishing date and authorship of canonical and extra-canonical documents, is highly questionable. Literary criticism as a discipline is highly speculative and is not acceptable as evidence in a court of law. In 1930, for example,[1] a Canadian citizen,

1. Details of this case are reported in a tape by Francis A. Schaeffer entitled, "Five problems with those who deny the Bible's evaluation concerning itself." This L'Abri Tape (no. 16) is available from: L'Abri Fellowship Foundation, Chalet Les Melezes, 1861 Huemoz, Switzerland.

Miss Florence Deeks, submitted a book for publication, entitled *The Web*, to Macmillan Co. in Canada. Although Miss Deeks' book, which was an outline of history, was never published, shortly thereafter H. G. Wells published his *Outline of History* through Macmillan Co. in England. Miss Deeks filed a lawsuit against H. G. Wells for plagiarism, asking $500,000 damages. The plaintiff's defense was made by the literary critic Professor Erwin, who found by the principles of literary criticism that the *Outline of History* that H. G. Wells had published could not possibly have been written independently, and that either it borrowed heavily from Miss Deeks' work, or both works were derived from a common third source. This conclusion was based upon the existence of numerous passages in both works which, although not identical, were similar to a certain extent in literary structure. According to the Ontario Law reports of 1931, the Honorable Mr. Justice Raimi ruled that evidence based upon literary criticism alone was unacceptable.[2]

---

2. Although evidence based upon literary criticism alone is inadmissible in a court of law, we shall see in the next chapter that in a court of law it is presumed that a document is genuine in its entirety until (admissible) evidence can be provided to the contrary. Just as it is the case (in order to insure that no innocent

Miss Deeks appealed her case, and the Honorable Justice Riddle of the Appelate Division of the Supreme Court of Ontario upheld Raimi's decision. Still dissatisfied, Miss Florence Deeks appealed to the Lords of the Privy council, highest tribunal of justice and the court of last resorts in the British Empire. The hearing lasted from October 1, 1932, until November 3, 1932, at which time, Lord Atkin, presiding justice, upheld the decisions of the other two courts, stating

---

man is convicted of a crime) that the accused is considered innocent until it can be proven on the basis of noncircumstantial evidence that he is guilty, so is it reasonable to require (in order to insure that no unjustifiable claims be made about the text) that the text be considered genuine in its entirety until historical or archaeological evidence is found to the contrary. Literary – critical methods, however, are highly speculative and lack uniformity in their results.

Therefore, in a court of law, the burden of proof would rest upon the one who has challenged the authenticity of the document. However, there are many who would find it very difficult to accept the authenticity of the New Testament, and who would desire that the burden of proof be left to the one who believes the New Testament to be genuine. For this reason, we will examine some of the indications of the authenticity of the New Testament from a literary point of view in a few of the following chapters. Many of the observations of those chapters are actually quite convincing, even though some of them are based upon literary considerations.

that evidence presented on the basis of literary criticism is inadmissible in a court of law. This case is mentioned in Irwin H. Linton's book, *A Lawyer Examines the Bible* (Grand Rapids, Michigan: Baker Book House, 1943), pp. 109-110.

5

Rules of Legal Evidence and the Documents of the New Testament

In a remarkable book, *The Testimony of the Evangelists*, Dr. Simon Greenleaf of Harvard Law School applies the laws of legal evidence to the New Testament accounts. The first rule of municipal law to which he alludes is as follows:

> Every document, apparently ancient, coming from the proper repository or custody, and bearing on its face no evident marks of forgery, the law presumes to be genuine, and devolves on the opposing party the burden of proving it to be otherwise.[1]

---

1. Simon Greenleaf, *An Examination of the Testimony of the Four Evangelists* (London: A. Maxwell & Son, 1847), p. 7.

He demonstrates the applicability of this rule to the New Testament documents, and notes that there is no pretense that they were engraven on plates of gold and discovered in a cave, nor that they were brought from heaven by angels, but that they are the plain narratives and writings of the men whose names they respectively bear, made public at the time they were written. The second rule that he cites is as follows:

> In matters of public and general interest, all persons must be presumed to be conversant, on the principle that individuals are presumed to be conversant with their own affairs.[2]

According to this rule, we must allow that in copying manuscripts, the Christians did not corrupt the text, since they must be presumed to be conversant with their own affairs. Now that we have fragments of manuscripts from as early as A.D. 130, we have excellent evidence that such a presumption is indeed justified.

The other rules of legal evidence are as follows:

> In trials of fact, by oral testimony, the proper inquiry is not whether it is possible

---

2. *Ibid.*, p. 8.

that the testimony may be false, but
whether there is sufficient probability that
it is true.[3]

A proposition of fact is proved, when its
truth is established by competent and
satisfactory evidence.[4]

In the absence of circumstances which
generate suspicion, every witness is to
be presumed credible, until the contrary
is shown; the burden of impeaching his
credibility lying upon the objector.[5]

The credit due to the testimony of witnesses depends upon, firstly, their hon-
esty; secondly, their ability; thirdly, their
number and the consistency of their testimony; fourthly, the conformity of their
testimony with experience; and fifthly, the
coincidence of their testimony with collateral circumstances.[6]

Greenleaf discusses each of these rules in
depth in relation to the New Testament.
Concerning the fifth point in the last of
these rules, he writes:

After a witness is dead, and his moral
character is forgotten, we can ascertain
it only by a close inspection of his nar-

---

3. *Ibid.*, p. 21.
4. *Ibid.*, p. 21.
5. *Ibid.*, p. 22.
6. *Ibid.*, p. 25.

rative, comparing its details with each other, and with contemporary accounts and collateral facts. This test is much more accurate than may at first be supposed. Every event which actually transpires, has its appropriate relation and place in the vast complication of circumstances, of which the affairs of men consist; it owes its origin to the events which have preceded it, is intimately connected with all others which occur at the same time and place, and often with those of remote regions, and in its turn gives birth to numberless others which succeed. In all this almost inconceivable contexture, and seeming discord, there is perfect harmony; and while the fact, which really happened, tallies exactly with every other contemporaneous incident related to it in the remotest degree, it is not possible for the wit of man to invent a story, which, if closely compared with the actual occurrences of the same time and place, may not be shown to be false.[7]

In another work entitled, "A Dissertation on Miracles," by George Campbell, principal of the Marshall College, Aberdeen, Scotland, written in correspondence between himself and David Hume, we read:

In a number of concurrent testimonies,

---

7. *Ibid.*, p. 25.

where there has been no previous concert [which is utterly negatived in the case of the Gospels by the apparent but completely reconciled discrepancies between them] there is a probability distinct from that which may be termed the sum of the probabilities resulting from the testimony of the witnesses; a probability which would remain even though the witnesses were of such character as to merit no faith at all. This probability arises from concurrence itself. That such a concurrence should spring from chance is as one to infinity; that is, in other words, morally impossible. If, therefore, concert be excluded, there remains no cause but the reality of the fact.[8]

William Paley wrote a book entitled *Horae Paulinae*, which was published in 1851 by Robert Carter & Brothers, New York. In this incredible study, he assumes the authenticity of neither the 13 letters of Paul nor the book of Acts, excludes considerations of any collateral evidence whatsoever and points out that agreement or conformity between letters bearing the name of an ancient author, and a received history of that author's life, does not necessarily establish the credit of either, since one may have been fabricated from the oth-

---

8. Irwin H. Linton, *op. cit.*, p. 55.

er. However, in the case of fabrication, conformity must be the effect of *design*, and vestiges will appear of such management or design. However, in examining the agreement between ancient writings, the character of truth and originality is undesignedness. Paley's book gives 260 pages of examples of how no design or contrivance has been imposed upon Paul's letters and the book of Acts to make them consistent. Paley writes:

> With respect to those writings of the New Testament which are to be the subject of our present consideration, I think that, as to the authenticity of the epistles, this argument, where it is sufficiently sustained by instances, is nearly conclusive; for I cannot assign a supposition of forgery, in which coincidences of the kind we inquire after are likely to appear.... As to the proofs of undesignedness, I shall in this place say little, for I had rather the reader's persuasion should arise from the instances themselves,... In a great plurality of examples, I trust he will be perfectly convinced that no design or contrivance whatever has been exercised; and, if some of the coincidences alleged appear to be minute, circuitous, or oblique, let him reflect that this very indirectness and subtilty is that which gives force and propriety to the example. Broad, obvious, and explicit agreements prove

little; because it may be suggested that the insertion of such is the ordinary expedient of every forgery: and, though they may occur, and probably will occur, in genuine writings, yet it cannot be proved that they are peculiar to these.... the description which St. Paul gives of himself in his Epistle to the Philippians (iii., 5)— "Circumcised the eighth day, of the stock of Israel, of the tribe of Benjamin, an Hebrew of the Hebrews; as touching the law, a Pharisee; concerning zeal, persecuting the Church; touching the righteousness which is in the law, blameless;"—is made up of particulars so plainly delivered concerning him in the Acts of the Apostles, the Epistle to the Romans, and the Epistle to the Galatians, that I cannot deny that it would be easy for an imposter, who was fabricating a letter in the name of St. Paul, to collect these articles into one view. This, therefore, is a conformity which we do not adduce. But, when I read, in the Acts of the Apostles, that, when "Paul came to Derbe and Lystra, behold a certain disciple was there, named Timotheus, the son of a certain woman *which was a Jewess*;" and when, in an epistle addressed to Timothy, I find him reminded of his "having known the Holy Scriptures *from a child*," which implies that he must, on one side or both, have been brought up by Jewish parents; I conceive that I remark a coincidence which shows, by its very *obliquity*, that scheme was not employed in its formation. In like manner, if a coincidence depend upon a comparison of dates, or rather of circumstances from which the dates are gathered—the more intricate that comparison shall be; the more numerous the intermediate steps through which the conclusion is deduced; in a word, the more *circuitous* the investigation is, the better, because the agreement which finally results is thereby farther removed from the suspicion of contrivance, affectation, or design. And it should be remembered, concerning these coincidences, that it is one thing to be minute, and another to be precarious; one thing to be unobserved, and another to be obscure; one thing to be circuitous or oblique, and another to be forced, dubious, or fanciful. And this distinction ought always to be retained in our thoughts.

The very particularity of St. Paul's epistles; the perpetual recurrence of names of persons and places; the frequent allusions to the incidents of his private life, and the circumstances of his condition and history; and the connection and parallelism of these with the same circumstances in the Acts of the Apostles, so as to enable us, for the most part, to confront them with one another; as well as the relation which subsists between the circumstances, as mentioned or referred

to in the different epistles—afford no
inconsiderable proof of the genuineness
of the writings, and the reality of the
transactions. For, as no advertency is
sufficient to guard against slips and con-
tradictions, when circumstances are mul-
tiplied, and when they are liable to be
detected by contemporary accounts equal-
ly circumstantial, an imposter, I should
expect, would either have avoided particulars entirely, contenting himself with
doctrinal discussions, moral precepts,
and general reflections; or if, for the sake
of imitating St. Paul's style, he should
have thought it necessary to intersperse
his composition with names and circumstances, he would have placed them out
of the reach of comparison with the history. And I am confirmed in this opinion
by the inspection of two attempts to coun-
terfeit St. Paul's epistles, which have
come down to us; and the only attempts,
of which we have any knowledge, that are
at all deserving of regard. One of these
is an epistle to the Laodiceans, extant in
Latin, and preserved by Fabricanus, in
his collection of apocryphal scriptures.
The other purports to be an epistle of St.
Paul to the Corinthians, in answer to an
epistle from the Corinthians to him. This
was translated by Scroderus, from a
copy in the Armenian language which had
been sent to W. Whiston, and was after-
wards, from a more perfect copy, pro-
cured at Aleppo, published by his sons,

as an appendix to their edition of Moses Chorenensis. No Greek copy exists of either; they are not only not supported by ancient testimony, but they are negatived and excluded; as they have never found admission into any catalogue of apostolical writings, acknowledged by, or known to, the early ages of Christianity. In the first of these I found, as I expected, a total *evitation* of circumstances. It is simply a collection of sentences from the canonical epistles, strung together with very little skill. The second, which is a more versute and specious forgery, is introduced with a list of names of persons who wrote to St. Paul from Corinth; and is preceded by an account sufficiently particular of the manner in which the epistle was sent from Corinth to St. Paul, and the answer returned. But they are names which no one ever heard of: and the account it is impossible to combine with any thing found in the Acts, or in the other epistles. It is not necessary for me to point out the internal marks of spuriousness and imposture which these compositions betray; but it was necessary to observe that they do not afford those coincidences which we propose as proofs of authenticity in the epistles which we defend.[9]

---

9. Blunt's *Coincidences* and Paley's *Horae Paulinae*, complete in one volume (New York: Robert Carter & Bros., 1851), part 2, pp. 8-13.

6

Eyewitness Testimony
in the New Testament

The writers of the New Testament documents appealed to themselves as observers of the events that they proclaimed. At the beginning of his first epistle, John states:

> That which was from the beginning, which we have heard, which we have seen with our eyes, which we have looked upon and touched with our hands, concerning the word of life—the life was made manifest, and we saw it, and testify to it, and proclaim to you the eternal life which was with the Father and was made manifest to us—that which we have seen and heard we proclaim also to you, so that you may have fellowship with us (1 John 1:1-3).

Appeal to eyewitness testimony abounds in the New Testament. In 2 Peter 1:16 we read:

For we did not follow cleverly devised myths when we made known to you the power and coming of our Lord Jesus Christ, but we were eyewitnesses of his majesty.

John, in his Gospel account, writes:

He who saw it has borne witness—his testimony is true, and he knows that he tells the truth—that you also may believe (John 19:35).

As we have seen, the authenticity of all these documents is extremely well attested. For example, it would be next to impossible to find a present-day scholar who denies the authenticity of Paul writing to the Corinthians in A.D. 55, where he says:

For I delivered to you as of first importance what I also received, that Christ died for our sins in accordance with the scriptures, that he was buried, that he was raised on the third day in accordance with the scriptures, and that he appeared to Cephas, then to the twelve. Then he appeared to more than five hundred brethren at one time, most of whom are still alive, though some have fallen asleep. Then he appeared to James, then to all the apostles. Last of all, as to one untimely born, he appeared also to me (1 Cor. 15:3-8).

In writing this letter, Paul leaves himself

wide open to cross-examination, exposing himself to the possibility of humiliation and censure should his claims prove to be false. It would certainly be a deterrent to his mission if his claim were found to be false by people cross-examining any of the five hundred witnesses to whom Paul refers.

Luke records in the book of Acts, that, when Peter and John were charged not to speak or teach at all in the name of Jesus, they answered:

> Whether it is right in the sight of God to listen to you rather than to God, you must judge; for we cannot but speak of what we have seen and heard (Acts 4:19, 20).

Other places in the book of Acts where there is appeal to eyewitness testimony are Acts 1:22, 2:22, 2:32, 3:15, 4:33, 5:32, 10:39, and 13:30, 31.

Not only is it the case that the early Christian writers appealed to eyewitness testimony concerning the events they had seen, but they appealed to the reader concerning his own knowledge of the events that had occurred. For example, at the beginning of his account, Luke writes:

> Inasmuch as many have undertaken to compile a narrative of the things which have been accomplished among us, just as they were delivered to us by those

who from the beginning were eyewitnesses
and ministers of the word, it seemed good
to me also, having followed all things
closely for some time past, to write an
orderly account for you, most excellent
Theophilus, that you may know the truth
concerning the things of which you have
been informed (Luke 1:1-4).

According to the book of Acts, Peter,
addressing the men of Judea and Jerusalem, stated:

Men of Israel, hear these words: Jesus
of Nazareth, a man attested to you by God
with mighty works and wonders and signs
which God did through him in your midst,
as you yourselves know . . . (Acts 2:22).

Appeal is made by Paul in Acts 26:26
to the awareness that king Agrippa had concerning the events that had occurred:

For the king knows about these things,
and to him I speak freely; for I am per-
suaded that none of these things has es-
caped his notice, for this was not done in
a corner.

It is clear, therefore, that the New Testament authors appealed not only to themselves as eyewitness of the events, but also
to the knowledge of the hearers and read-
ers concerning the events that had occurred among them.

A. T. Olmstead, in discussing the eyewitness testimony offered by John in his Gospel concerning the resurrection of Lazarus, writes:

> Such is the story originally told by John and with all the circumstantial detail of the convinced eyewitness. It is utterly alien in form to the literary miracle tale.[1]

Concerning the resurrection of Jesus and John's testimony, Olmstead writes:

> This is the story of the empty tomb—told by an undoubted eyewitness—full of life, and lacking any detail to which the skeptic might take justifiable objection.[2]

> This likewise is the testimony of a convinced eyewitness; if modern scholars do not accept the vision as objective reality, the blame should be laid on the psychologist and not the historian.[3]

> Such is the outline of the resurrection appearances as we can reconstruct from our sources the earliest accounts. Our picture may not be quite exact, but it cannot be far wrong. These stories must have originated within a few days after the discovery of the empty tomb, and have been written down within the first few years

---

1. A. T. Olmstead, *Jesus in the Light of History* (New York: Charles Scribner's Sons, 1942), p. 206.

2. *Ibid.*, p. 248.

3. *Ibid.*, p. 249.

after the organization of the primitive church. Otherwise, it is quite impossible to understand the survival of the empty tomb story so unnecessary to confirm their own faith after the full acceptance of the resurrection, or the still more amazing survival of those constant doubts of the disciples themselves, for to invent them only a few years later would have been a public scandal.

Of one thing we may be sure: the appearances cannot be reckoned as mere literary devices. Not only do they betray their primitive character, they do not hesitate to relate to their discredit the doubts of their church leaders, written down and circulated while those leaders were yet living and able if they wished to refute them.[4]

---

4. *Ibid.*, p. 251.

7

The Appeal to Belief and Its Significance

One characteristic that separates the New Testament accounts from most accounts of legend or mythology is that the skepticism of the people is portrayed in detail and emphasis is placed upon belief. The fact that these writers should be concerned with belief at all is quite interesting, for it is minimal, if not nonexistent, in most accounts of legend or mythology. The emphasis upon belief is an indication that the New Testament authors were totally convinced that they were writing completely valid historical accounts. If they did not believe what they were writing, then they were lying with the specific purpose of deception, fully conscious of what they were doing, in a malicious attempt to manipulate the people of their day. One certainly cannot suppose that the people of Christ's time had a propensity for believing in the miraculous. Such an emphasis as exists in the New Testament upon belief would be totally unnecessary and out of place if that were the case. The account of what occurs in connection with the belief of the people is incredibly realistic. There were people who believed but were too afraid to let it be known (John 12:42 and 19:38). The people described are true to life. It would be only natural that people would doubt the claims of Christ, and this is exactly how they are represented (see John 2:18, 6:30, 6:42, 8:51-53, 20:25; Acts 7:51, 4:3, 4; 1 Cor. 15:12). The characters are not two dimensional; they do not lack depth. Peter loses his faith after the arrest of Jesus (John 18:17). He is quite human—he has nothing in common with the modern stereotype of the naïve peasant living two thousand years ago who is willing to believe whatever he is told. Nor is this stereotype valid concerning most of the other people mentioned in the New Testament. Their depth of personality is very well portrayed by the writers of these accounts.

8

The Testimony of Ignatius

Ignatius of Antioch was born in about
A.D. 30. Most of the information that we
have concerning him is contained within
his seven letters, the authenticity of these
being extremely well attested (see J. B.
Lightfoot, *The Apostolic Fathers*, edited
and completed by J. R. Harmer (London
1891); Kirsopp Lake, *The Apostolic Fathers* (Loeb Classical Library, New York
1912); K. Bihlmeyer, *Die apostolischen
Väter* (Tübingen 1924); J. H. Strawly, *The
Epistles of Saint Ignatius* (S.P.C.K., London
1935)). He was martyred when he was
thrown to the beasts in the Flavian amphitheatre in Rome in the second half of the
reign of the Emperor Trajan (A.D. 98-117).
There is reason to suppose that he came
into contact with more than one of the Apostles. In fact, in the third chapter of his letter

to the Smyrnæans we read:

> As for me, I know that even after His resurrection He was in the flesh, and I believe this to be true. For, when He came to those who were with Peter, He said to them: "Take hold on me and handle and see that I am not a spirit without a body." And, as soon as they touched Him and felt His flesh and pulse, they believed. It is for this reason that they despised death and even showed themselves superior to death. After His resurrection He ate and drank with them like anyone else with a body, although in His spirit He was one with the Father.

> (Ignatius of Antioch, Epistle to the Smyrnæans, chapter 3, reprinted in Francis Glimm, *The Apostolic Fathers* (Washington: The Catholic University of America Press, 1962), p. 119.)

From this letter, it can be seen that Ignatius was probably intimately acquainted with those who were with Peter when this occurred, and that they had described to him these events.

9

The Testimony of the Changed
Lives of the Early Christians

One strong indication of the historicity
of the resurrection is the changed lives of
the early Christians. These men were
transformed from utter cowardice to what
would appear to be complete foolhardiness.
Consider some of the indications of the
cowardice of these men before the resurrection:

First, at the capture of Jesus, when
Judas betrayed Him, "all the disciples for-
sook him and fled" (Matt. 26:56 and Mark
14:50).

Second, Peter denied Jesus three times
for fear of being indentified as a disciple
of Jesus (John 18:15-27, Mark 14:66-72, Luke
22:54-62). Luke writes:

Then they seized him and led him away,

bringing him into the high priest's house. Peter followed at a distance; and when they had kindled a fire in the middle of the courtyard and sat down together, Peter sat among them. Then a maid, seeing him as he sat in the light and gazing at him, said, "This man also was with him." But he denied it, saying, "Woman, I do not know him." And a little later some one else saw him and said, "You also are one of them." But Peter said, "Man, I am not." And after an interval of about an hour still another insisted, saying, "Certainly this man also was with him; for he is a Galilean." But Peter said, "Man, I do not know what you are saying." And immediately, while he was still speaking, the cock crowed. And the Lord turned and looked at Peter. And Peter remembered the word of the Lord, how he had said to him, "Before the cock crows today, you will deny me three times." And he went out and wept bitterly

Third, John records that the disciples were afraid of the Jews, and were hiding in an upper room behind closed doors:

On the evening of that day, the first day of the week, the doors being shut where the disciples were, for fear of the Jews, Jesus came and stood among them and said to them, "Peace be with you" (John 20:19).

After the resurrection, these very same men were proclaiming what they had seen and heard to the point of endangering their lives. In the book of Acts, Luke records that John and Peter (who out of fear had previously denied Jesus three times) were completely unafraid even when confronted with the highest officials, including "Annas the high priest and Caiaphas and John and Alexander, and all who were of the high-priestly family" (Acts 4:6). Luke writes:

> Now when they saw the boldness of Peter and John, and perceived that they were uneducated, common men, they wondered; and they recognized that they had been with Jesus. But seeing the man that had been healed standing beside them, they had nothing to say in opposition. But when they had commanded them to go aside out of the council, they conferred with one another, saying, "What shall we do with these men? For that a notable sign has been performed through them is manifest to all the inhabitants of Jerusalem, and we cannot deny it. But in order that it may be spread no further among the people, let us warn them to speak no more to any one in this name." So they called them and charged them not to speak or teach at all in the name of Jesus. But Peter and John answered them, "Whether it is right in the sight of God to listen to you rather than to God, you must judge;

> for we cannot but speak of what we have
> seen and heard" (Acts 4:13-20).

These people became the active nucleus of
a group of people who began to defy the
Sanhedrin and boldly accuse it of crucifying
its own Messiah (Acts 2:23 and 4:10).[1] Despite imprisonment and harassment, the
leaders remained in Jerusalem instead of
fleeing to the greater security of Galilee.
The small group of disciples which had met
in an upper room behind closed doors began
a bold campaign to proclaim Jesus' messiahship in the very city in which He had
been condemned to death.[2]

In John 7:5 we find that "even his brothers did not believe in him." Yet after the
resurrection, "all these with one accord devoted themselves to prayer, together with
the women and Mary the mother of Jesus,
and with his brothers" (Acts 1:14). James,
one of the brothers of Jesus (Mark 6:3),
after being confronted with the risen Christ
(1 Cor. 15:7), went on to write this in his
epistle: "James, a servant of God and of

---

1. Merrill C. Tenney, *The Reality of the Resurrection* (New York: Harper and Row, 1963), p. 135.

2. Merrill C. Tenney, "The Resurrection of
Jesus Christ" in Carl F. H. Henry, *Prophecy in the
Making* (Carol Stream, Ill.: Creation House, 1971),
p. 61.

the Lord Jesus Christ, To the twelve tribes in the dispersion: Greeting" (James 1:1).

These people were so certain of the resurrection that they were willing to die rather than deny it. Luke records the stoning of Stephen as he proclaimed the messiahship of Jesus in Acts 7:51-60. Many of the eleven apostles died heinous deaths as martyrs proclaiming the events they had witnessed.[3]

The conversion of Paul has for long been regarded as a weighty evidence for the truth of Christianity.[4] Lord George Lyttleton wrote that "The conversion and apostleship of St. Paul alone, duly considered, was of itself a demonstration sufficient to prove Christianity to be a divine revelation." [5]

---

3. *Encyclopaedia Americana,* under the articles on each individual apostle.

4. F. F. Bruce, *op. cit.*, p. 77.

5. George Lyttleton, Letter to Gilbert West, reprinted in Gilbert West and George Lyttleton, *A Defence of the Christian Revelation,* 1748. This volume contains Gilbert West's celebrated *Observations on the History and Evidences of the Resurrection of Jesus Christ* as well as Lyttleton's *Observations on the Conversion of St. Paul,* of which Dr. Samuel Johnson said:

He had, in the pride of juvenile confidence, with the help of corrupt conversation, entertained doubts of the truth of Christianity; but he thought the time now come when it was no longer fit to doubt or believe by chance, and applied himself seriously

Also called Saul of Tarsus (Acts 13:9), Paul studied under Gamaliel (Acts 22:3), the grandson of Hillel, and was a man commanding great respect among the Jewish leaders of his time. Even the ruling authorities respected his great learning:

> And as he thus made his defence, Festus said with a loud voice, "Paul, you are mad; your great learning is turning you mad." But Paul said, "I am not mad, most excellent Festus, but I am speaking the sober truth. For the king knows about these things, and to him I speak freely; for I am persuaded that none of these things has escaped his notice, for this was not done in a corner (Acts 26:24-26).

Saul was responsible for the persecution and death of many Christians (Acts 8:1-3; 9:1, 2; 22:4, 5). We read:

> But Saul, still breathing threats and murder against the disciples of the Lord, went to the high priest and asked him for

---

to the great question. His studies being honest, ended in conviction. He found that religion was true; and what he had learned he endeavoured to teach (1747) by *Observations on the Conversion of St. Paul*; a treatise to which infidelity has never been able to fabricate a specious answer.

This quote from Dr. Samuel Johnson, according to F. F. Bruce, *op. cit.*, p. 77, is from *Lives of the Poets: Lyttleton*.

letters to the synagogues at Damascus,
so that if he found any belonging to the
Way, men or women, he might bring
them bound to Jerusalem (Acts 9:1, 2).

Suddenly, he began proclaiming that he had
seen the risen Christ on the road to Damascus (Acts 22:6-11, 26:12-18), and became the
key apostle in the growth of the early Christian Church. He was tortured beyond belief
during his ministry, but he still insisted
upon his testimony. In 2 Corinthians 11:23-28, he writes:

> Are they servants of Christ? I am a better
> one—I am talking like a madman—with
> far greater labors, far more imprisonments, with countless beatings, and often
> near death. Five times I have received at
> the hands of the Jews the forty lashes less
> one. Three times I have been beaten with
> rods. . . .

These events are described in Acts 16:22-24, 14:19, and 9:23, 24. He was finally persecuted under Nero in A.D. 64.[6]

Secular sources admit that this dramatic
change occurred in Paul's life.[7] Although
such sources often treat the explanation as
unknown, Paul's explanation, recorded in

---

6. *Encyclopaedia Britannica* (1965), vol. 14, p. 984.

7. *Encyclopaedia Britannica* (Chicago: William
Benton, 1973), vol. 17, p. 470.

the book of Acts, is as follows:

"I am a Jew, born at Tarsus in Cilicia, but brought up in this city at the feet of Gamaliel, educated according to the strict manner of the law of our fathers, being zealous for God as you all are this day. I persecuted the Way to the death, binding and delivering to prison both men and women, as the high priest and the whole council of elders bear me witness. From them I received letters to the brethren, and I journeyed to Damascus to take those also who were there and bring them in bonds to Jerusalem to be punished.

"As I made my journey and drew near to Damascus, about noon a great light from heaven suddenly shone about me. And I fell to the ground and heard a voice saying to me, 'Saul, Saul, why do you persecute me?' And I answered, 'Who are you, Lord?' And he said to me, 'I am Jesus of Nazareth whom you are persecuting.' Now those who were with me saw the light but did not hear the voice of the one who was speaking to me. And I said, 'What shall I do, Lord?' And the Lord said to me, 'Rise, and go into Damascus, and there you will be told all that is appointed for you to do.' And when I could not see because of the brightness of that light, I was led by the hand by those who were with me, and came into Damascus" (Acts 22:3-11).

The account is given by Luke in Acts 9:1-19 and is given by Paul as quoted by Luke in Acts 26:9-18, as well as in Acts 22:3-11 quoted above. Paul's letter to the Galatians (1:11-17) also describes this event.

Secular historians do not doubt the historicity of the book of Acts, but the attempt is often made to find alternative explanations for many of the events recorded, such as the conversion of Paul. For example, the *Encyclopaedia Britannica* attempts to explain Paul's conversion by claiming that it had been the last stage of a long preparatory process.[8] However, this explanation does not square with the primary source materials, including Paul's own letters. The change was too sudden. It is certain that the overnight transformation from one extreme to the other would not have occurred had a preparatory process been involved.

---

8. *Ibid.*, pp. 469-472.

10

Circumstantial Evidences for the
Resurrection of Christ*

All four Gospels agree that Jesus died
(or "yielded up his spirit") when he was
on the cross (Matt. 27:50, Mark 15:37, Luke
23:46, John 19:30). In Mark 15:39 we read,
"And when the centurion, who stood facing
him, saw that he thus breathed his last,
he said, 'Truly this man was the Son of
God!'" The centurion's use of the past
tense indicates that he considered Jesus
dead. Through his experiences as a centurion on the battlefield and at executions,
he was well qualified to determine whether
Jesus had merely fainted or had actually
died.[1]

---

*The material in this chapter is adapted from a
speech given by Josh McDowell at the University of
Rochester in the spring of 1971.
1. Merrill C. Tenney, *The Reality of the Resurrection* (New York: Harper and Row, 1963), p. 106.

The soldiers standing guard over the victims did not break His legs to hasten death because He was already dead (John 19:33).

In Mark 15:43-45, we read:

> Joseph of Arimathea, a respected member of the council, who was also himself looking for the kingdom of God, took courage and went to Pilate, and asked for the body of Jesus. And Pilate wondered if he were already dead; and summoning the centurion, he asked him whether he was already dead. And when he learned from the centurion that he was dead, he granted the body to Joseph.

Certainly, the friends of Jesus who buried Him were certain that He was dead, or they would not have wrapped the body in graveclothes and entombed Him as they did (Luke 23:53).

John, in his Gospel, records that one of the soldiers who came to take Jesus off the cross pierced His side with a spear, and that at once there came out blood and water (John 19:34).[2]

From these considerations, it can be seen that there is no uncertainty concerning the death of Jesus.

---

2. See Merrill C. Tenney, "The Resurrection of Jesus Christ" in Carl F. H. Henry, *Prophecy in the Making* (Carol Stream, Ill.: Creation House), p. 51.

It is interesting to investigate the circumstantial evidences concerning the resurrection. We are told in John 19:39 that Christ was wrapped in cloth containing 100 pounds of spices. Such practice was not unusual among Jews for entombment during that period. For example, Gamaliel (who was the grandson of Hillel, the great Jewish scholar who was born in Bethlehem) was a contemporary of Jesus who was buried in 80 pounds of spices.[3] The custom was to put the body on a stone slab, straighten the members, and wrap the body with a linen cloth about 30 centimeters wide, putting the spices mixed with a gummy substance between the folds. The body would be wrapped up to the armpits, then wrapped from the fingertips to the neck, using a separate shroud for the head. After a few hours, the graveclothes would harden, forming an encasement around the body.[4]

After Jesus was wrapped in graveclothes and placed in the tomb, a large stone was rolled against the entrance of the tomb (Matt. 27:60). When such a tomb

---

3. Michael Green, *Man Alive!* (Downers Grove, Ill.: Inter-Varsity Press, 1967), p. 33.

4. Merrill C. Tenney, *The Reality of the Resurrection* (New York: Harper and Row, 1963), p. 117.

was vacant, the stone was held at one side
by a cleat or small block placed beneath
it. After a body was placed in a tomb the
cleat was removed, and the stone settled
into place, covering the door completely.[5]

Mark 16:4 refers to the stone as extremely large. Papias, an extrabiblical
source writing in A.D. 90 records from
all historical accounts that Mark was cor-
rect and accurate in recording everything
that Peter said and had seen.[6] Being
aware of the sizes of the entrances to such
tombs, which are 4 1/2 to 5 feet high, we
know that the stone must have weighed
between 1 1/2 and 2 tons.[7]

In Matthew 27:62-66, we read:

> Next day, that is, after the day of Prep-
> aration, the chief priests and the Phari-
> sees gathered before Pilate and said,
> "Sir, we remember how that impostor
> said, while he was still alive, 'After three
> days I will rise again.' Therefore order

5. *The Reality of the Resurrection, op. cit.,* pp.
110-111.
6. Eusebius, *Historica ecclesiastica,* III. 39., reprinted in Roy J. Deferrari, *Eusebius Pamphili Ecclesiastical History* (New York: Fathers of the
Church, Inc., 1953), p. 206.
7. See Josh McDowell, *Evidence That Demands A
Verdict* (San Bernardino, Cal.: Campus Crusade for
Christ, Inc., 1972), pp. 215-217.

the sepulchre to be made secure until the
third day, lest his disciples go and steal
him away, and tell the people, 'He has
risen from the dead,' and the last fraud
will be worse than the first." Pilate said
to them, "You have a guard of soldiers;
go, make it as secure as you can." So
they went and made the sepulchre secure
by sealing the stone and setting a guard.

The Greek Word *koustodia* is used for
"guard" in this context. The word *koustodia* is used again in Matthew 28:11-15:

While they were going, behold, some of
the guard went into the city and told the
chief priests all that had taken place.
And when they had assembled with the
elders and taken counsel, they gave a
sum of money to the soldiers and said,
"Tell people, 'His disciples came by night
and stole him away while we were asleep.'
And if this comes to the governor's ears,
we will satisfy him and keep you out of
trouble." So they took the money and did
as they were directed; and this story has
been spread among the Jews to this day.

It is significant that it was necessary that
the *governor* be satisfied, because there
is no account in history, secular, Jewish
or Christian, that the Roman governor had
anything at all to do with the temple police.
Yet critics will claim that the temple police
guarded the tomb, rather than the official

Roman guard. The reason that they came to the high priest was that they knew that the high priest had influence with the Roman government. The Romans were afraid of a Jewish revolt, and they wanted good relations with the Jewish leaders. Furthermore, we have the ancient Oxyrhynchus papyrus from A.D. 22 which uses the Greek word *koustodia* for the Roman guard.[8]

Flavius Flagidius Renaultus was a Roman military historian who recorded the methods of offensive and defensive warfare used by the Romans. According to the Military Classics Series, these methods are still used by the U.S. Government for the training of the Green Berets. According to Flagidius, a *koustodia* was a 16-man security unit, each man of which was trained to protect six square feet of ground. With 16 man square (four on each side), they were able to protect 96 square feet of ground against an entire invading army, and hold it. Pliny (the Roman statesman and author), Sutonious, Casitus, and Flavius Josephus, the Jewish historian— all indicate that the enemy tremendously feared the Roman guard. If one man in

---

8. A. T. Robertson, *Word Pictures in the New Testament* (New York: R. R. Smith, Inc., 1931), p. 239.

the Roman guard failed in his duty, he was automatically executed along with the other fifteen men, each being stripped of his clothes and burned alive in a fire started by their own garments. The members of the *koustodia* were well aware of the punishment that awaited all of them if just one fell asleep or left his position.[9]

According to Matthew, the *koustodia* was placed at the tomb, and a seal was put on the tomb. According to A. T. Robertson, this could only refer to the Roman seal. The *koustodia* was there to protect the seal. According to Flagidius, wherever the Roman seal was placed, the premises were thoroughly examined and the Roman guard was to protect it, for the seal stood for the power and authority of the Roman Empire. The people feared the breaking of the seal. The tomb was sealed by stretching a cord across the stone and fastening it to the rock of the tomb at both ends by means of sealing clay stamped with the Roman imprint at either end. When the seal was broken, all the Roman officials and authorities would search for the offender, and when found, he would be crucified.[10]

---

9. From a speech delivered by Josh McDowell at the University of Rochester, spring of 1971.
10. *Ibid.*

Anybody who attempts to explain away the resurrection of Christ must explain the breaking of the much feared Roman seal, the disappearance of the Roman guard, the rolling away of the stone in front of the tomb, and the disappearance of the body from the graveclothes which remained (John 20:3-8).

The stone, according to Matthew, was rolled (*apokulio*) away from the tomb (Matt. 28:2). Mark uses the same root (*kulio*), using the preposition *ana*, which means "up" or "upward" (Mark 16:4). The phrase *anakulio* can only mean to roll something up a slope or an incline. For Mark to have used that phrase, there had to be a slope or an incline coming down to the entrance of that tomb. Matthew and Luke both use the root *kulio* with the preposition *apo*, which means "away" from something —setting a separation or sense of distance (Matt. 28:2 and Luke 24:2). The phrase *apokulio* can only mean to roll one object from another object with the sense of distance. Thus, the stone was rolled, and at a distance from the opening of the tomb.[11]

In Mark 16:1-4, we read:

And when the sabbath was past, Mary

11. Josh McDowell, *Evidence That Demands A Verdict* (San Bernardino, Cal.: Campus Crusade for Christ, Inc., 1972), p. 231.

80

Magdalene, and Mary the mother of James, and Salome, brought spices, so that they might go and anoint him. And very early on the first day of the week they went to the tomb when the sun had risen. And they were saying to one another, "Who will roll away the stone for us from the door of the tomb?" And looking up, they saw that the stone was rolled back; for it was very large.

The women lived in Bethlehem. Christ had been buried Friday. They left Friday night and did not return until Sunday morning. The Roman guard had been placed Saturday morning, but the women had not been informed of this, having been in Bethlehem. According to the above quote, the women looked *up* to see that the stone was rolled back. Furthermore, in saying, "Who will roll away the stone for us from the door of the tomb?" (Mark 16:3), they used the Greek word for the *entrance* of the tomb, which would have been logical. But when they arrived at the tomb, the word they used was the Greek word for the entire massive sepulchre, rather than the entrance as before (see Luke 24:2). The Greek word *airo* is used in John 20:1, which means to pick up something and carry it away.

After the resurrection, there was never

any question as to the emptiness of the tomb. That it was empty was easily verifiable by a four-minute walk from Jerusalem. The debate centered around the question as to why the tomb was empty.

After the resurrection, the Roman authorities were anxious to put a stop to the spread of Christianity, which they thought was causing a disturbance. Yet it would have been an easy matter for them to have stopped it had they only produced the body of Christ. Yet they were never able to produce it.[12]

Another impressive consideration in dealing with the resurrection is the character and moral integrity of the witnesses. It would have been totally inconsistent for these people to have conspired for the purpose of a deception if they themselves had only a portion of the moral integrity that we know they had. (See Pliny the Younger, Book X, xcvi to Emperor Trajan, A.D. 112.) According to this secular source they would "bind themselves by oath, not for any criminal purpose, but to abstain from theft, robbery and adultery, to commit no breach of trust and not to deny a deposit when called upon to restore it."

---

12. From a speech delivered in spring of 1971 by Josh McDowell.

A further consideration is discussed by
Merrill C. Tenney:

> It is noteworthy that these appearances
> are not stereotyped. No two of them are
> exactly alike. The appearance to Mary
> Magdalene occurred in early morning (Jn.
> 20:1); that to the travelers to Emmaus
> in the afternoon (Lk. 24:29); and to the
> apostles in the evening, probably after
> dark (Lk. 24:36). He appeared to Mary
> in the open air (Jn. 20:14). Mary was
> alone when she saw Him; the disciples
> were together in a group; and Paul re-
> cords that on one occasion He appeared
> to more than five hundred at one time
> (I Co. 15:6). The reactions were also
> varied. Mary was overwhelmed with
> emotion (Jn. 20:16-17); the disciples
> were frightened (Lk. 24:37); Thomas was
> obstinately incredulous when told of the
> Lord's resurrection (Jn. 20:25), but wor-
> shiped Him when He manifested Him-
> self (20:28). Each occasion had its own
> peculiar atmosphere and characteris
> tics, and revealed some different quality
> of the risen Lord.[13]

There is no question of the material
reality of the appearances. In two cases,

---

13. Merrill C. Tenney, "The Resurrection of Jesus
Christ" in Carl F. H. Henry, *Prophecy in the Making*
(Carol Stream, Ill.: Creation House, 1971), p. 59.

He ate with those to whom He appeared (Luke 24:41-43 and John 21:13. See also Acts 10:41). Jesus exhibited His wounds in Luke 24:39-40 and John 20:27, and invited closer inspection. An illusion cannot eat and cannot be inspected by several persons at will.[14]

None of the descriptions is fanciful or stilted. He acts like a normal human being, except for the unusual ability to appear and disappear at will. Each time Christ appeared it was for a definite purpose. He appeared to restore Peter, to comfort Mary, to dispel the doubts of Thomas, and to give renewed hope to the frustrated and disillusioned pair that were walking to Emmaus.[15]

Various theories have been advanced to explain away the resurrection, but the circumstantial evidences that we have cited preclude the tenability of any of these theories. For example, a few centuries ago, Venturini advanced a theory according to which Jesus never really died on the cross. But even the skeptic, D. F. Strauss, writes that "it is impossible that a being

---

14. *Ibid.*, p. 59.

15. *Ibid.*, p. 60. See also Wilbur M. Smith, *Therefore, Stand: Christian Apologetics* (Grand Rapids: Baker Book House, 1968), p. 388.

who had stolen half dead out of the sepulchre, who crept about weak and ill, wanting medical treatment ... could have given to the disciples the impression that he was a Conqueror over death and the grave, the Prince of Life, an impression which lay at the bottom of their future ministry. Such a resuscitation ... could by no possibility have changed their sorrow into enthusiasm, have elevated their reverence into worship." [16]

16. David F. Strauss, *The Life of Jesus for the People*, Eng. trans., 2nd ed. (London: Williams and Norgate, 1879), I, 412.

11

The Change of Sabbath as Evidence for Christ's Resurrection*

One monumental indication of the resurrection of Christ concerns the Sabbath. In the first few years of Christianity, all the Christians were Jews (Acts 10:45, 11:18). The Jewish Sabbath has always been kept on Saturday, the seventh day of the week. Yet the early Christians, who were Jewish, met for worship on the first day of the week, Sunday. This was considered the Lord's Day (Rev. 1:10), because Jesus had been resurrected on the first day of the week (Mark 16:9, Luke 24:1-7, John 20: 1, 19).

---

*Although the research in this chapter is original, most of the references used are the same as those originally cited by Charles DeLoach in *The Armstrong Error* (Plainfield, N.J.: Logos International, 1971), chapter VII, "The Christian and the Sabbath."

86

The practice of assembling together on the first day of the week began the week after Christ's resurrection had taken place (John 20:26). The practice of gathering together on the first day of the week is also mentioned in Acts 20:7 and 1 Corinthians 16:2.

To change a tradition such as the day of sabbath among Jews would ordinarily have been exceedingly difficult. The Jewish sabbath day is observed in obedience to the fourth commandment, "Remember the sabbath day, to keep it holy. Six days you shall labor, and do all your work; but the seventh day is a sabbath to the LORD your God; in it you shall not do any work, you, or your son, or your daughter, your manservant, or your maidservant, or your cattle, or the sojourner who is within your gates; for in six days the LORD made heaven and earth, the sea, and all that is in them, and rested the seventh day; therefore the LORD blessed the sabbath day and hallowed it" (Ex. 20:8-11).

The letter of Ignatius of Antioch to the Magnesians, chapter 9, refers to observation of the Lord's Day rather than the traditional Sabbath, in honor of Christ's resurrection:

How, then, shall we be able to live apart from Him, seeing that the prophets were

His disciples in the Spirit and expected Him as their Master, and that many who were brought up in the old order have come to the newness of hope? They no longer observe the Jewish Sabbaths, but keep holy the Lord's day, on which, through Him and through His death, our life arose. . . .[1]

This letter to the Magnesians is one of seven letters written by Ignatius of Antioch before he was thrown to the beasts in the Flavian amphitheatre in Rome in the second half of the reign of Emperor Trajan (A.D. 98-117).[2]

The Epistle of Barnabas, chapter 15, also mentions this practice:

This is why we also observe the eighth day with rejoicing, on which Jesus also rose from the dead, and having shown himself ascended to heaven.[3]

The Epistle of Barnabas, it is agreed

---

1. Ignatius of Antioch, "Epistle to the Magnesians," chapter 9, reprinted in Francis Glimm, *The Apostolic Fathers* (Washington: The Catholic University of America Press, 1962), pp. 98-99.

2. Francis Glimm, *The Apostolic Fathers* (Washington: The Catholic University of America Press, 1962), p. 84.

3. Epistle of Barnabas, chapter 15, reprinted in Edgar J. Goodspeed, *The Apostolic Fathers* (New York: Harper and Brothers, 1950), p. 41.

among scholars, could not have been written later than A.D. 150 and might have been written as early as A.D. 70 or 71.[4]

In the *Apology to Caesar* of Justin the Martyr, chapter 67, we read:

> But Sunday is the day on which we all hold our common assembly, because it is the first day on which God, having wrought a change in the darkness and matter, made the world; and Jesus Christ our Saviour on the same day rose from the dead.[5]

Justin Martyr died in A.D. 165, when he suffered martyrdom in the reign of Marcus Aurelius, according to *Chronicon Paschale.*[6]

In the *Didache*, or the *Teaching of the Twelve Apostles*, we read:

> And on the Lord's Day, after you have come together, break bread and offer the Eucharist, having first confessed your offences, so that your sacrifice may be pure.[7]

4. Francis Glimm, *op. cit.*, p. 187.

5. Justin Martyr, *The First Apology*, chapter LXVII, reprinted in Alexander Roberts, *Ante-Nicene Christian Library* (Edinburgh; T. and T. Clark, 1867), vol. II, p. 66.

6. Alexander Roberts, *Ante-Nicene Christian Library* (Edinburgh: T. and T. Clark, 1867), vol. II, p. 3.

7. *The Didache*, 14:1, reprinted in Francis Glimm,

The *Didache* was held in great repute by the early church, and was probably in circulation among the churches prior to A.D. 70.[8]

In his *Ecclesiastical History*, Book III, chapter 27, Eusebius wrote:

> They observed the sabbath and the rest of the discipline of the Jews just like them, but on Sundays they performed ceremonies like ours in commemoration of the Lord's Resurrection. Therefore, because of such practices they received their name, since the name of Ebionites signifies the poverty of their understanding, for the poor man is called by this name among the Hebrews.[9]

Pliny the Younger, whom Trajan had sent to govern the province of Bithynia in Asia Minor, wrote in a letter in A.D. 112 to the Roman Emperor about the practice of Christians in Bithynia on this "fixed day":

> they had met regularly before dawn on a

The Apostolic Fathers (Washington: The Catholic University of America Press, 1962), p. 182.

8. Jean-Paul Audit, *La Didachè Instructions Des Apôtres* (Prais: Libraire Lecoffre, 1958), pp. 187-210.

9. Eusebius Pamphili, *Ecclesiastical History*, Book III, chapter 27, reprinted in Roy J. Deferrari, *Eusebius Pamphili Ecclesiastical History* (Washington: The Catholic University of America Press, 1953), p. 184.

fixed day to chant verses alternately among themselves in honour of Christ as if to a god, and also to bind themselves by oath, not for any criminal purpose, but to abstain from theft, robbery and adultery, to commit no breach of trust and not to deny a deposit when called upon to restore it.[10]

As can be seen from these examples, references from early sources concerning the practice of the first Christians, most of whom were Jewish, establish that they had established the first day of the week as the sabbath day in commemoration of the resurrection. It would be extremely difficult to find any other explanation for this abrupt change in the tradition of these people.

---

10. Plinius Caecilius Secundus, C., Ep. X. 96, reprinted in Betty Radice, Pliny *Letters and Panegyricus* (Cambridge, Mass.: Harvard University Press, 1969), p. 289.

12

The Biblical Conception
of Resurrection

There are at least four specific references to a bodily resurrection of the dead
in the Old Testament:

Isaiah 25:8—He will swallow up death
for ever, and the Lord GOD will wipe
away tears from all faces . . .

Isaiah 26:19—Thy dead shall live, their
bodies shall rise. O dwellers in the dust,
awake and sing for joy! . . .

Ezekiel 37:12, 13—Therefore prophesy,
and say to them, Thus says the Lord
GOD: Behold, I will open your graves,
and raise you from your graves, O my
people; and I will bring you home into
the land of Israel. And you shall know
that I am the LORD, when I open your
graves, and raise you from your graves,
O my people.

Daniel 12:2—And many of those who
sleep in the dust of the earth shall
awake, some to everlasting life, and
some to shame and everlasting contempt.

References to the resurrection of the
dead abound in the New Testament. Seven specific examples follow:

Luke 14:14—You will be repaid at the
resurrection of the just.

John 6:40—For this is the will of my
Father, that every one who sees the Son
and believes in him should have eternal
life; and I will raise him up at the last
day.

Acts 26:8—Why is it thought incredible
by any of you that God raises the dead?

1 Corinthians 6:14—And God raised the
Lord and will also raise us up by his
power.

2 Corinthians 4:14—knowing that he who
raised the Lord Jesus will raise us also
with Jesus and bring us with you into
his presence.

John 5:28, 29—Do not marvel at this: for
the hour is coming when all who are in
the tomb will hear his voice and come
forth, and those who have done good,
to the resurrection of life, and those who
have done evil, to the resurrection of
judgment.

Acts 24:15—having a hope in God which these themselves accept, that there will be a resurrection of both the just and the unjust.

Three references, Daniel 12:2 from the Old Testament plus John 5:28, 29 and Acts 24:15 from the New Testament, refer to a resurrection of both the just and the unjust.

The resurrection of Christ gave assurance to the early Christians that they also would be resurrected:

1 Peter 1:3—we have been born anew to a living hope through the resurrection of Jesus Christ from the dead.

1 Thessalonians 4:14—For since we believe that Jesus died and rose again, even so, through Jesus, God will bring with him those who have fallen asleep.

1 Corinthians 15:12—Now if Christ is preached as raised from the dead, how can some of you say that there is no resurrection of the dead?

1 Corinthians 6:14—And God raised the Lord and will also raise us up by his power.

2 Corinthians 4:14—knowing that he who raised the Lord Jesus will raise us also with Jesus and bring us with you into his presence.

According to the New Testament, the resurrection of Christ also provides assurance that He will judge the world:

Acts 17:31—because he has fixed a day on which he will judge the world in righteousness by a man whom he has appointed, and of this he has given assurance to all men by raising him from the dead.

In fact, the resurrection of Christ is central as an epistemological basis for the validity of Christianity:

1 Corinthians 15:14, 17—if Christ has not been raised, then our preaching is in vain. . . . If Christ has not been raised, your faith is futile.

Jesus is considered the "first fruits" of the resurrection:

Romans 8:29—For those whom he foreknew he also predestined to be conformed to the image of his Son, in order that he might be the first-born among many brethren.

Colossians 1:18—He is the head of the body, the church; he is the beginning, the first-born from the dead, that in everything he might be pre-eminent.

Hebrews 1:6—And again, when he brings the first-born into the world, he says, "Let all God's angels worship him."

Revelation 1:5—and from Jesus Christ the faithful witness, the first-born of the dead, and the ruler of kings on earth.

1 Corinthians 15:20, 23—But in fact Christ has been raised from the dead, the first fruits of those who have fallen asleep. . . . But each in his own order: Christ the first fruits, then at his coming those who belong to Christ.

According to the New Testament, we have been provided with information concerning the nature of our resurrection bodies by having observed Christ's resurrection body:

Philippians 3:21—who will change our lowly body to be like his glorious body, by the power which enables him even to subject all things to himself.

1 John 3:2—when he appears we shall be like him.

Thus, the following information concerning the resurrection body of Jesus is applicable to our own resurrection bodies:

Luke 24:36-43—As they were saying this, Jesus himself stood among them. But they were startled and frightened, and supposed that they saw a spirit. And he said to them, "Why are you troubled, and why do questionings rise in your hearts? See my hands and my feet, that it is I myself;

handle me, and see; for a spirit has not flesh and bones as you see that I have." And while they still disbelieved for joy, and wondered, he said to them, "Have you anything here to eat?" They gave him a piece of broiled fish, and he took it and ate before them.

It seems, from this passage, that Jesus materialized before the very eyes of these people, startling them and frightening them. However, He demonstrated that He was not a spirit, and that He could eat and be touched. Thus, although tangible, He could pass through closed doors as He did in John 20:19, where He materialized before the disciples:

John 20:19—On the evening of that day, the first day of the week, the doors being shut where the disciples were, for fear of the Jews, Jesus came and stood among them and said to them, "Peace be with you."

Christ's body had also passed through the graveclothes in which He was wrapped. In John 19:39 we find that Christ was wrapped in graveclothes containing 100 pounds of spices:

John 19:39, 40—Nicodemus also, who had at first come to him by night, came bringing a mixture of myrrh and aloes about a hundred pounds' weight. They took the

body of Jesus, and bound it in linen
cloths with the spices, as is the burial
custom of the Jews.

Yet in John 20:6-8 the linen cloths were
left lying in such a way as to cause John
to believe that Christ had indeed been resurrected. Had the linen cloths been un-
wrapped, John would undoubtedly have
thought the body to have been removed
from the tomb:

John 20:6-8—Then Simon Peter came,
following him, and went into the tomb;
he saw the linen cloths lying, and the
napkin, which had been on his head, not
lying with the linen cloths but rolled up
in a place by itself. Then the other disciple, who reached the tomb first, also
went in, and he saw and believed.

The following references also describe the
resurrection body:

Romans 8:23— . . . as we wait for adoption
as sons, the redemption of our bodies.

2 Corinthians 5:1-4—For we know that if
the earthly tent we live in is destroyed,
we have a building from God, a house
not made with hands, eternal in the heav-
ens. Here indeed we groan, and long to put
on our heavenly dwelling, so that by putting it on we may not be found naked.
For while we are still in this tent, we
sigh with anxiety; not that we would be

unclothed, but that we would be further
clothed, so that what is mortal may be
swallowed up by life.

1 Corinthians 15:42-44, 51-55—So is it
with the resurrection of the dead. What is
sown is perishable, what is raised is imperishable. It is sown in dishonor, it is
raised in glory. It is sown in weakness, it
is raised in power. It is sown a physical
body, it is raised a spiritual body.... Lo!
I tell you a mystery. We shall not all
sleep, but we shall all be changed, in a
moment, in the twinkling of an eye, at the
last trumpet. For the trumpet will sound,
and the dead will be raised imperishable,
and we shall be changed. For this perishable nature must put on the imperishable,
and this mortal nature must put on immortality. When the perishable puts on
the imperishable, and the mortal puts on
immortality, then shall come to pass the
saying that is written: "Death is swallowed up in victory. O death, where is thy
victory? O death, where is thy sting?"

According to the New Testament accounts, Jesus, during His ministry, often
predicted that He would be raised from the
dead (see John 10:17; Luke 9:22, 11:29, 30,
16:31, 18:33; Mark 8:31, 9:9, 9:31, 10:34,
14:28; Matt. 16:4, 16:21, 17:9, 17:23, 20:19,
26:32, 27:63). He offered His future resurrection as validation for His extensive
claims concerning himself. He claimed to

have authority to forgive sins (Luke 5:20, 21, 24), and to be Teacher and Lord (John 13:13). He claimed that apart from himself, one could do nothing (John 15:5). He said, "I am the resurrection and the life; he who believes in me, though he die, yet shall he live" (John 11:25). He claimed that He would come again at the close of the age (Mark 13:26). He claimed to be the Messiah prophesied in the Old Testament (see John 1:49-51 and 4:26). He claimed to be equal with God (John 5:18). This is not surprising since at least seven Old Testament passages equate the coming Messiah with God (Ps. 45:6, 7; Isa. 9:6, 7:14; Micah 1:3; Zech. 14:9; Isa. 44:6 compared to Job 19:25, Mal. 3:1). For example, in Isaiah 9:6 we find the following prophecy concerning the Messiah to come: "For to us a child is born, to us a son is given; and the government will be upon his shoulder, and his name will be called Wonderful Counselor, *Mighty God*, Everlasting Father, Prince of Peace" (italics added).

Christ claimed that these extensive claims concerning himself would be validated by His resurrection from the dead. For example, after asserting His authority in such a way as to imply that He was the expected Messiah, the Jews were angry and demanded proof:

John 2:18-21—The Jews then said to him, "What sign have you to show us for doing this?" Jesus answered them, "Destroy this temple, and in three days I will raise it up." The Jews then said, "It has taken forty-six years to build this temple, and will you raise it up in three days?" But he spoke of the temple of his body.

See also Matthew 12:39-41 as an example of Christ's reference to His eventual resurrection as the validation for His claims about himself.

One corollary to the resurrection of Christ which is implicit in the New Testament is that it put the stamp of authority on everything that Jesus said and did. Furthermore, another interesting corollary to the resurrection of Christ implicit in the New Testament is that Christ's resurrection validates the claims of the Old Testament concerning itself, to which Jesus subscribed. Jesus treated all of the Old Testament as that which had occurred in space, time and history. That Jonah was swallowed by a great fish is treated as historical fact by Jesus in Matthew 12:39-41. That a flood destroyed everybody on earth except Noah and his family is treated by Jesus as historical fact in Luke 17:26-30. That God spoke to Moses through the burning bush in history is asserted by Jesus in Mark 12:24-27. However, Jesus asserted that, "If they do not hear Moses and the prophets, neither will they be convinced if some one should rise from the dead" (Luke 16:31).

13

Conclusion: The Resurrection
of Christ vs. Speculation

Most people have undergone the experience of reasoning something out and
reaching a conclusion which has later prov-
en to be false. Men, being fallible, are capable of committing errors in logic without realizing that they have done so. Even
if one's argument should be perfectly
sound, one may begin with invalid presuppositions. Such is the nature of speculation. When men speculate, they are susceptible to error either in choosing their
presuppositions or in the structure of the
argument employed. While one is susceptible to such error in the process of speculation, one may never discover the mistakes in one's argument.

Christianity is unique as a system of

thought in that it claims to be based upon historical event rather than upon a complex of philosophical presuppositions.[1] If the history recorded in the New Testament documents has actually occurred, then it is no longer necessary for us to continue speculating, for God has given us a direct indi-

---

1. Although it is possible to raise the objection that Judaism, as system of thought, *also* claims to be based upon historical event, it must be understood that Christianity is not confronted with counterclaims in the historical events upon which Judaism is based. On the contrary, the historical events described in the Hebrew scriptures constitute part of the history upon which Christianity itself is based. Nor should we expect that Mormonism, for example, would affect the uniqueness of this claim. Although Mormonism claims to be based upon certain historical events not found in the Canon, it nevertheless affirms the historicity of both the Hebrew scriptures and the New Testament.

Whether or not there are any other systems of thought claiming to be based upon historical event, it can nevertheless be said that any system of thought which is based upon nothing more than philosophical presuppositions will always be susceptible to the possibility of error. This susceptibility to error results from the possibility of beginning with invalid presuppositions. The frailty of such systems can be understood when one realizes that there are many philosophical systems which, although fairly self-consistent, cannot be reconciled with one another. Christianity, however, claims to be based upon something more than mere speculation, and if its claims are true, the implications are overwhelming.

cation of what we would like to know concerning the purpose for man's existence and concerning his destiny beyond the grave.

One is much more easily convinced of something by the shock of being confronted with a man who has returned from the grave (and who has made extensive claims concerning himself and the rest of the universe), than he is by the conclusion of a process of reasoning which is subject to error.

If I were to convince myself that a proposition were true on the basis of reason (which is susceptible to error), and if somebody claimed that I was wrong (and that, being equal to God, he knew everything), I might not take him seriously. But if he claimed that he would come back from the grave in order to validate his claims, and if later he were to do just that, I would be convinced that my conclusion was based upon faulty reasoning, even if I were not yet aware of the specific errors in reasoning that I have committed. Of course, I would have to be certain that he has indeed returned from the dead. Yet the evidence is overwhelming that Jesus was resurrected. In the face of the evidence, it is certainly the case that it takes more faith to believe, against the evidence, that the resurrection did not occur, than it does to believe that it has occurred.

One presupposition that is widely held in the twentieth century is that of uniformity of natural causes in a closed system, according to which the possibility of any event occurring in such a way as to be contrary to observed laws of nature is excluded before examination of any evidence to the contrary. One must consider whether it is valid to make such a presupposition in the face of as much contrary evidence as exists. Certainly, on the basis of the data we have examined, it would be safer to presuppose a uniformity of natural causes in an open system.

One might ask how it would be possible that one can be resurrected if he has had, through the slow process of change, several different bodies throughout his lifetime. One answer is that it would be dangerous to equate personal identity (which is suggested by continuity of consciousness and persistence of personality) with bodily identity. In 1 Corinthians 15:51 we are told that "we shall be changed" at the resurrection. To conclude, on the basis of mere speculation, that the biblical concept of resurrection is impossible, or that there is no such thing as private identity, is very dangerous in consideration of the monumental historical evidence for the resurrection of Christ which has been presented. One must be willing to admit that we do not have all the answers, and that God in His omnipotence is not going to be restrained by our feeble attempts to understand the world in which we live. Philosophical speculation is susceptible to error. If Christ was resurrected, then we have something more concrete than speculation upon which to base our contentions.

OTHER QUALITY BOOKS FROM BETHANY FELLOWSHIP

_____Christian Perfection, by Fenelon $1.95

_____The Working of the Holy Spirit in Daily Life,
    by Sister Eva of Friedenshort $1.25

_____Beyond Humiliation, by J. Gregory Mantle . $1.95

_____Wholly for God, by William Law/
    Andrew Murray $2.75

_____The Life of God in the Soul of Man,
    by Henry Scougal $1.50

Buy them at your local bookstore or order direct by checking
the book you want and filling out the coupon below:

**BETHANY FELLOWSHIP, INC. Dept. DS, 6820 Auto
Club Rd. Minneapolis, MN 55438**

Please send me the books I have checked above. I am enclosing
$_____ (Please add 35c to cover postage and handling.) Send
check or money order—no cash or C.O.D.'s please.

Mr./Mrs./Miss _____

Address _____

City _____ State _____ Zip _____

Check here _____ if you would like a free book catalog